# STILL
# KICKING

# STILL KICKING

## RUTH A. WILLIS

XULON PRESS

Xulon Press
2301 Lucien Way #415
Maitland, FL 32751
407.339.4217
www.xulonpress.com

© 2021 by Ruth A. Willis

Contribution by Charles Willis, Dr. Mervyn Warren

All rights reserved solely by the author. The author guarantees all contents are original and do not infringe upon the legal rights of any other person or work. No part of this book may be reproduced in any form without the permission of the author.

Due to the changing nature of the Internet, if there are any web addresses, links, or URLs included in this manuscript, these may have been altered and may no longer be accessible. The views and opinions shared in this book belong solely to the author and do not necessarily reflect those of the publisher. The publisher therefore disclaims responsibility for the views or opinions expressed within the work.

Unless otherwise indicated, Scripture quotations taken from the King James Version (KJV)–*public domain*.

Paperback ISBN-13: 978-1-66283-500-1
Ebook ISBN-13: 978-1-66283-501-8

This story is being written:
July 22, 2020
By: Ruth Ann Willis

Advisor: Dr. Mervyn A Warren: Huntsville, Alabama
A special thanks for the ones who were the readers for of my story:
Mary Trendt: Westfield, Indiana
Kindra Lynnette Henderson: Atladena California
Doris Young: Indianapolis, Indiana

There are several reasons I have chosen to write my autobiography. The main reason I have written my story is because of my life experiences.
The title for my story was suggested by our oldest daughter Crystal Ann Willis-Jones.
Title: "Still Kicking"

The bible verse that fits my story is:
Psalm 23:1: The Lord is my Shepard I shall not want.

This Story is dedicated to my husband of 47 years, Charles Milton Willis and our two daughters Crystal Ann and Sharone Ellen Willis.

Ruth Ann Willis

# Table of Contents

*≈≈≈≈≈≈≈≈≈*

*Introduction* ............................... xi

Chapter 1:   Tough Times .................... 1

Chapter 2:   Twist and Turns ................ 19

Chapter 3:   An Unexpected turn of Events ... 23

Chapter 4:   So Many Lessons to Learn ....... 27

Chapter 5:   A Loss ......................... 33

Chapter 6:   My Search ...................... 43

Chapter 7:   Time for a new Experience ...... 53

Chapter 8:   A New Experience ............... 57

Chapter 9:   A life Changing Decision ....... 61

Chapter 10:  Never say Never ................ 65

Chapter 11:  A Friendship to Treasure ....... 73

Chapter 12: Setting a Wedding Date .........79

Chapter 13: Becoming a Wife ...............83

Chapter 14: Starting Life as Mr.
and Mrs. Charles Willis .........89

Chapter 15: Our Time at Oakwood..........95

Chapter 16: Our Time at Andrews
University....................103

Chapter 17: Partnership with Jesus
In Lake Region Conference.....109

Chapter 18: Charles Teaching at
Peterson Warren...............113

Chapter 19: A Time for Change ............119

Chapter 20: After Retirement .............131

*Preface*

# CHOICES

There always are ifs in life:

What if I had chosen to allow myself to take on the lifestyle of my biological parents' addiction to alcohol my life would have been totally different.

What if I had allowed the people that surrounded me to determine my destiny. What if I had decided not to allow God to order my steps in the direction He had for me.

God has always lovingly watched over me and my siblings, to whom, I am very grateful.

Over the years I have learned to recognize, that everything happens for a reason. The experiences in life can help you to trust God or to distrust Him. Our struggles made us more determined to succeed. Our situation could have destroyed any desire we might have had to succeed. For us the desire to survive was stronger than our will to give up as children.

I want to acknowledge Charles as a powerful influence in my life over the past 47/48 years of marriage. Charles testimony as a Christian is what attracted me to him. Charles has never been ashamed to let others know how important God is in his life. There are so many times men are fearful of letting anyone know that they believe in Christ. I thank God that my life companion loves the Lord.

# Introduction

There can be many challenges in life that can destroy our reason to believe there is a way to overcome all the obstacles in our families and communities. No one can overcome unless they allow the Lord to take over all the negative challenges that we ourselves cannot handle. As the soccer ball in my story gets kicked around we also get kicked around, many times by people we have grown to trust with our lives. You may have grown up in an environment that has made you think that you are product of your family situation. Try to make your resolve to not allow the negative situations control your future. God has a plan for all of our lives and we must allow Him to direct our paths. I would not say that there will not be struggles. Our lives can be so much better when we allow the Lord to control our destiny. I have written my story because of my experience as a child and as an adult. There is nothing impossible when we allow God to have control of our lives.

*Chapter 1*

# TOUGH TIMES

~~~~~~~~~~~~~~

Normally a life story begins with I was born on this day, so that is the way I will begin. I was born July 10, 1944 during the 2$^{nd}$ World War. Life was not so easy, at that time or after the war. There have always been serious problems in the social, economic, and environmental world, as far as I have been able to tell. During the war and after the war nothing was for sure, and nothing is for sure at this time. From my observation there are still wars and hurting people.

From 1920 to 1933, there was the prohibition on alcoholic beverages. After 1933, people were allowed to purchase alcohol with no problem. More people have indulged in drinking these toxic beverages since it has become legal. Because of the free indulgence of these beverages, there have been a lot more broken homes. The addiction to alcohol has brought about a different sort of poverty. This type of drink has become the cause of financial ruin for many people that were otherwise considered successful.

Today, there is a problem with the use of marijuana and other drugs. It just takes one time for a person to have an immediate addiction to crack. Those who have had one experience with drugs of any form keep looking for that first high. The people who suffer most are the children, from parental addictions to drugs.

I was born in a house on Bemis St. in Grand Rapids, Michigan. The day I was born I was told both of my parents were drunk. I was told the doctor who delivered me was also intoxicated. My daughters have suggested that my birthday could have been on July 4, 1944, instead of July 10th

1944 as there was no original record of my birth. Since my parents were both drunk and I was born in a house, that is why, I believe my birthdate was just a guess.

My biological father was Scott Sylvester King. I don't know a lot about him. I do know he was a draftsman and an alcoholic with untreated high blood pressure. It is my understanding that he was born in South Bend, Indiana.

My biological mother was Beatrice Jane King born in Pensacola, Florida. I have no information regarding her maiden name but it is believed, to have been Birdie.

I had one sister, Jane Beatrice, who was born at Cook County Hospital in Chicago on (May 4, 1943). Janie was one year older than me. I have one brother Scott Sylvester, who was born at Saint Mary's Hospital in Grand Rapids, Michigan on (November 11, 1946). My brother is 2 years younger than I am. We called our brother Sonny, because of his happy disposition. I can't remember much about my biological parents. The one thing

I do remember is that our parents were alcoholics. Our mother would leave the home and go on binges, with anyone, who would drink with her. My father would leave us with our aunts, (Vera Banister or Aunt Mable, I can't remember Mable's last name) to go and try to find our mother. There were so many times, he would find her on the street or in jail. I do remember one time our father took us to St. Mary's Hospital in Grand Rapids, Michigan. We could see our mother looking from a window, on the rehabilitation floor. Our parents decided to make a change, so we started going to the church on the corner of Bemis street. After a few months the lure of alcohol became too strong, our mother went back to drinking. Our mother would always leave the home, and our father would leave us with our aunts and would always go to try and find her. She would either on the street or in jail.

Our father decided to get an account at the local liquor store thinking that our mother would stay home. Scott soon found that the liquor store account wasn't accomplishing what he thought it would. This account only put a financial burden on him. He eventually couldn't pay the store account and lost his job, and the house and we were forced to move.

*My sister Janie had the long braids, and I'm the little girl behind the baby*

I had started kindergarten, when I was 4 ½ (1948 or 1949) at Henry Elementary School in Grand Rapids, Michigan. My teacher Mrs. Scott was a very loving and caring person. Some days she would pick me and my sister up for school.

Sometime in September, 1949 things began to change drastically. Because of the financial situation, our family we moved to the southwestern part of Michigan, the Berrien County, nothing was the same. Before our father found jobs on migrant farms in that area. Our family moved in with friends in a section in Benton Harbor, Michigan that was called the Flats (where the black community lived). We slept on the floor of their friend's homes.

During this time our mother still indulged in drinking as much as she had before. Our mother would leave our family for three or four days, sometimes a week on alcoholic binges. A few days after our mother would leave our father would go and search for her. She would either be with people who were drinking with her or she would be in jail. Scott also drank heavily and was not able to provide for his family. I believe that they in their own strange way loved us, but the temptation to drink was stronger than their love for us.

The first migrant farm Scott found a job, the owner was not prepared for us. The farmer didn't have a place for us to stay. The famer had a tractor barn where he would keep supplies. He had cots that he set up outside for us to sleep on (I was 5 and a half then. I went to sleep on one of the cots. Sometime during the night a blue razor was at the head of my cot, getting ready to strike me in the head. Scott heard the snake and killed it. I was told about the snake the next morning.

There was a vacant shack that was made available for us after the incident with the snake. Several days after this situation our mother left and Scott went to find her.

Being left alone without parents and going hungry was something we became accustomed to. We would get food wherever we could find it. This was a very difficult time for our family, but especially for us as children. As children we just couldn't understand what was going on. We became much like the soccer ball that was being kicked around by the player. We were without any control over our lives, because we were too young.

Scott in his feeble efforts to try to keep us together would work as a migrant farm laborer. The only housing available for migrant workers were one room shacks. This was our situation, wherever he would find a job, a one room shack is where we lived. After Scott would find a job, our mother would once again leave for three or four days, and he would go and try to find her. During these times, we were left with strange men, whom we did not know. Looking back at our lives, I can still visualize the situation we were in. There was nothing pretty about how we lived or where we lived. We were in a very sad situation as children without parents, who wanted to take care for them.

I promised myself, that if I ever had children, they would never go through what we went through.

The first time the State of Michigan took us from our parents, I was 6 ½ years old. We were left alone the farmer reported our condition to the state. The truant officer took us to a foster home. The lady's name was Mrs. Johnson (1950) in Benton Harbor. We were with Mrs. Johnson for about four months while our parents tried to get themselves together.

When the state of Michigan officials recognized that our parents were in a better situation, returned us to them. Everything seemed to be going fine for a few months, but the lure of alcohol was stronger than our parents desire to keep us. Our father would get jobs on farms, and at first everything was going fine our mother was home. Our mother would only need to get one drink and she would leave and find people who would drink with her. Alcohol was a very real weakness for her. Following the pattern our father would go to try and find her. He'd be gone for three or four days. Sad to say once again we were left without anything except to live in a one room shack and go hungry.

Once again, it was reported to the state of Michigan that we were left alone. The state once again took us back to Mrs. Johnson in Benton Harbor, Michigan. This time we were with Mrs. Johnson for six months. Then our parents got themselves together and this time they had a house for us to live in and we were happy. We started to go to school in Sodus, Michigan. At the Sodus Elementary School we had begun making friends, but once again there was another disappointment. This time we watched them, in desperation for alcohol, drink wood alcohol (rubbing alcohol). Our parents had no control over their desire for alcohol. They were addicted to it. Their desire for alcohol was as strong as people who are addicted to crack or cigarettes. They drank wood alcohol as though we weren't watching them.

We have never been able to get over the kind of hurts we faced. The hurts, we faced caused us to struggle with low self-esteem. We did not know how to cope with constant disappointments, defeats, and failures that seemed to surround us.

There was the feeling of constantly being abandoned and deserted by those who had the power to fulfill your needs, but didn't. The soccer ball is a true representative of how we were kicked around, by anyone who saw our condition. We were dirty and raggedy and we were treated as lepers in the bible. We had nothing.

The main concern Janie and I had was, for our younger brother. Sonny was three and ½ years old at the time. One day we were walking on a country road, he cut his foot on a tin can and the cut was untreated. Our father was in a drunken stupor, and did nothing to take care of his foot. Sonny to this day at age 74 still has the scars from the cut.

Sonny reminded me of the room behind a barber shop in Benton Harbor, off Main Street, that had bugs and rats. We stayed in this place in between our father finding jobs. A rat tried to bite Sonny's foot. He is still terrified of the bugs and the rats to this day. Sonny's memory of our biological parents is not pleasant he doesn't want anyone to call him (Scott). My brother prefers to be called Sonny.

There were so many places we lived in that were unacceptable. I can also remember the place behind the barber shop. My brother recently talked to me about that place, it was one room with a bed and was dirty. He doesn't want a relationship with any of the King family. Some members of King Family have tried to reach out to us now that we are older. Even though they didn't know our condition, our thoughts are for them to leave us alone as they had done when we were growing up. We were deserted by the King family and the hurt is still there.

Because Janie was the oldest, she had to endure the majority of the disappointments.

In life trials come and go, but wanting and needing security just didn't happen. For us at that point in our lives, it appeared those things never seemed to be something we could expect in our early years. We had no friends or family who would say, I think I have some clothes or shoes you can have. No one said you can take a bath at our house or you can eat at our table.

We could have been angry and have taken our anger and frustration out on others that would not have helped us. Our situation was so very painful to this day the pain is still there. The best way to understand it is to believe that God was in control of our lives even though we did not know Him. It would have helped if we had known how to pray, but that was not our privilege. We were orphans, without parents who would have had our best interest at heart. We were at the mercy of those around us. We were without friends or family.

REPORT OF COUNTY WELFARE AGENT TO:     HON. MALCOLM HATFIELD
                                       PROBATE JUDGE

IN THE MATTER OF:           KING, Jane      10, 5- 4-43
                                  Ruth Ann   8, 7-10-44
                                  Scott, Jr. 7,11-11-48

                            Petition Dated: Dec. 9, 1953

                            Parents: Scott King
                                     Beatrice King
                            Address:

These children were referred to this Court at this present time by
a petition which was signed by the _____ wife of the farmer
on who's place they were living in a shack. This petition signed
Dec. 9, 1953 set forth the following allegations:

> "The above named children are being neglected by their
> parents. The mother has abandoned them. The father
> drinks and is unable to give them the proper care.
> They do not have sufficient food and clothing."

This was the second petition filed in this Court on the neglect
of these children.    The first petition was signed on the 3rd of
December, 1952 and set forth the following allegations:

> "Mother left this family two months ago and has never returned.
> The father was given money for food for the children but
> would spend it for drink. Last Sunday, November 30, this
> father left and has not returned, leaving these children in
> a shack in which there was no stove nor food.  The children
> have been taken care of by a colored man in his shack.
> These children should be placed in a good home where they
> could have the security to which they are entitled."
>                          a year ago
At the time this petition was filed/last December, the mother had
been gone for some time, and the father finally took the children
5,8, and 9 to the home of another colored man, and left them, and
he, too, disappeared.   This colored was totally unable to care
for the children and, therefore, the landlord signed the petition
dated December, 3, 1952.   At that time the children were taken
and placed in a boarding home until a hearing could be had.   Due
to the abject neglect of these children by their parents, it was
presumed the children would be removed permanently from the custody
of the parents, but in a short time, the parents had gotten together
and appealed to this Court for the return of the child.  They had
managed to get a new place to live and work, which was on
a farm in Coloma.  It being near Christmas, an investigation
of their new home was made, and it was found that they were living in
an adequate house which was kept clean and neat by the mother who
was sewing and mending and who promised to keep the home and the
children in good condition.  The father was working every day in the
orchards trimming trees.  Everything seemed to be all right, and the
children were returned to them on condition that this type of living
continued.

Shortly after this, Mr. King again took to drinking some and the
house was not kept as neat as it had been.  Minor complaints came
in from time to time from his employer about his drinking and not
working.  Soon, however, these complaints stopped.

Again about the same time this year just before Christmas, complaints
again were brought to this court about the mother having left home
and the father lying around drunk almost all of the time.  On the
9th day of December, 1953, Petitioner signed a petition to this effect
and a call was made to the home.  I found the most deplorable conditions
imaginable.  The father and children had been eating out of the same

Page #2   KING CHILDREN

dishes without even washing them. The two small beds were covered with filthy rags for warmth. The place was dirty beyond description. One of the girls reportedly was sleeping with her father while the boy was sleeping with the other sister, which in itself did not look good. And the mother, up to her old habit, had deserted the family long before this time. It was reported to me that the way the family got anything in the way of fire wood or food was to steal it while most of the money was spent on drink. The children were left alone much of the time even all night without heat.

The children were removed into a boarding home once more and clothing was obtained for them. Their underthings were in shreds which were barely hanging on the children. Not one word has been heard from the parents. In attempting to serve summons on the parents, I was told by person after person that they had moved to their farm only to be evicted because they were not desirable tenants. The last report was that they were living in Berrien County, but no one knew where. It was then decided to advertise in order to serve on the parents.

RECOMMENDATION: It is recommended that these children be made permanent wards of this court and consent be given to their adoption by the Judge of this Court.

COUNTY AGENT

Dated:   January 14, 1954

| 1. Given First Name of Adopted Person at Birth | |
|---|---|
| "Ruth" | |
| 2. Date, time, and place of birth of adopted person: | |
| 7/10/1944, at Grand Rapids, Michigan | |
| 3. Ethnicity, racial background of birth Mother: | 3a. Ethnicity, racial background of Father: |
| African American | African American |
| 4. Religious Background of Birth Mother | 4a. Religious Background of Birth Father |
| Unknown | Unknown |
| 5. General Description of Birth Mother | 5a. General Description of Birth Father |
| Not provided. | Not provided. |
| 6. Age of Birth Mother at Time of Termination of Parental Rights | 6a. Age of Birth Father at Time of Termination of Parental Rights |
| 46 years of age. | 51 years of age. |
| 7. Age and Sex of Siblings of Adopted Person at Time of Adoption | |
| Two full siblings. Girl, 11 years of age; boy, 8 years of age. | |
| 8. Length of Time Parents Married at Time of Placement | |
| Unknown | |
| 9. Education/Occupation of Birth Family | |
| Unknown | |
| 10. Hobbies/Special Interests of Birth Family | |
| Information not provided. | |
| 11. Status of Termination | |
| ☐ Voluntary      ☒ Court Ordered | |
| 11a. Circumstances of Court Ordered Termination of Parental Rights of Birth Parents | |
| Neglect | |
| 12. Length of Time Between Termination of Parental Rights and Child's Placement | |
| Parental rights were terminated 2/1/54. You were placed in the adoptive home on 4/19/1954. | |
| 13. Account of Health, Psychological and Genetic History of Child | |
| Early medical information is not available in the file. At the time of placement in the adoptive home, you were in good health. | |
| 14. Account of Health and Genetic History of Birth Parents and Other Members of Child's Family | |
| Birth parents were said to be heavy drinkers. The father claimed to have ulcers of the stomach brought on by drinking heavily. | |
| 15. If Parent is Deceased, the Cause of and Age at Death | |
| N/A | |
| 16. Past Relationships of Adopted Person | |
| None | |
| Other Information: | |
| Your adoption was finalized by the Berrien County Probate Court, 3/30/1955. | |

PETITION—Juvenile Court—(Act 54 of Extra Session of 1944)    P250—(Rev. 1944)    12-522

# State of Michigan,

CAUSE No. 5820

### The Probate Court for the County of Berrien

Juvenile Division.

In the Matter of the Petition Concerning **Jane, Ruth Anne, and Scott, Jr., King**

MINOR.

I, **Petitioners**, respectfully represent that I reside in the _____ of **Watervliet** _____ in said County, and make this petition as **interested party**

I further represent that said **children are residents of** ~~is a resident of the~~ **Watervliet** in **Berrien** County, and is now residing with and under the custody and control of **father** and _____ was born on **and Scott was born 11-11-45** Jane was born 3-1-43; Ruth Ann was born 7-10-44

I further represent upon information and belief that said child **ren** ~~on or about, to-wit, the _____ day of _____ A.D.19____ , in said County of_____~~

* **are being neglected by their parents. The mother has abandoned them. The father drinks and is unable to give them the proper care. They do not have sufficient food and clothing**

I further represent that the names, relationship, ages and residences of nearest of kin and guardian of said child_____, as I am informed and believe, are as follows:

| NAME | RELATIONSHIP | AGE | RESIDENCE |
|---|---|---|---|
| Scott King | father | | |
| Beatrice King | mother | | |

I therefore, pray that the Juvenile Court take jurisdiction of said child.

(Signed) **Petitioners**

P. O. **Watervliet, Mich.**

Subscribed and sworn to before me this **9th** day of **December** A. D. 19 **53**, at **Watervliet**, Michigan.

(Signed) **Thomas Starkey**
Notary Public, **Berrien** County, Michigan.
My commission expires **February 26** 19 **56**.

A preliminary inquiry having been made from which it appears that the interest of the public and said child require that formal jurisdiction be acquired by this Court, therefore the filing of the foregoing petition is hereby authorized.

Dated **Dec. 9-53** (SEAL) **MALCOLM HATFIELD**
Judge of Probate.

Filed **9th** day of **December** A. D. 19 **53**.

**Hazel Gallsmith**
Probate Register, Juvenile Division.

* Here allege the facts.

*Chapter 2*

# TWIST AND TURNS

But then, as my story goes the alcohol was stronger once again, we wound up living in another one room shack. I remember one day my brother, my sister and I were walking down a country road, singing" We Ain't Got a Barrel of Money, Maybe we're Ragged and Funny, but we're side by side". We were abandoned we didn't know what to do to change our situation.

On the last migrant farm we went to a one room school. We were fortunate in that they served hot lunches. There was no food, no water, and no one to see that we had proper clean clothes in the shack we lived in. We were ragged, smelly and didn't know what condition we were really in.

For fun, we played in the mud outside our shack. Some days Janie and I would try to clean the shack and make it look nice. That did not work it was still a shack.

Our parents had disappeared for more than 2 weeks. The farmer's wife tried to look out for us and she finally contacted the State of Michigan. One Friday when we got out of school, there was a truant officer at the school to pick us up. He took us to another foster home in Benton Harbor, Michigan. The foster mother's name was Daisy Atkins. While we were with Mrs. Atkins, we started going to Bard Elementary School. I was so messed up that I failed the second grade twice. I felt like I was in some type of stupor. Sad to say my IQ was 70 which was nothing to be proud of. Living in an unstable situation didn't help any. I wasn't able to read or write. I really wanted to know how to do those things and comprehend these tools in my education.

It was horrible being left and not being able to even understand the reason why you were born. The questions I had about my existence went unanswered. There was no parental guidance for our lives or any goals set.

This was a real struggle that was very hard to understand or even talk about until now. There was no one to answer the hurt and disappointment of being abandoned. It seemed all the other children had a home and their biological parents. Sometimes, I would cry and say to myself maybe our parents will come and get us. This hope died after six months. I would think: how could they leave us like this. We were their children and we loved them.

There will always be an empty void that no matter how much money you have or high your position, or how much education you get, that void will always be there. I am thankful that there were and that still are people who will open their homes those in need. Foster parents are a great treasure to our society, because they are willing to share their lives and their homes.

On Sundays, we would go to the Baptist Church on Main Street in Benton Harbor. Mrs. Atkins, (we called her mother Atkins) had a son, Don who became a minister in the 2nd Baptist church. Don became like an older brother to us. Mother Atkins was very proud of her son.

*Chapter 3*

# An Unexpected turn of Events

Daisy Atkins had some friends she wanted to introduce us to. Some of her friends planned a dinner at the Dumas Hotel in Benton Harbor, where we met William and Ora Murdock. After we were introduced to the Murdocks' they wanted to visit with us at their home. The following Sunday we were invited to their house for dinner. The Murdock's didn't have any children and they wanted to adopt two children a boy (my brother) and a girl (my sister) they only wanted 2 children. After meeting us, they thought about it and they decided that they didn't want to separate us so they decided to take me also. I knew that adopting me was not in their plan. I would have been happy even if they had decided not to adopt me. I wanted my brother and sister in a safe place without the kind of life stress we had been facing with our biological parents.

*Pictured are William and Ora Murdock*

In 1954 the Murdocks petitioned the state of Michigan for permission to adopt all three of us. The adoption was completed in 1955. We were happy, to have a home and parents that made life somewhat better. The feeling of being deserted was a feeling that is hard to explain to people who have never experienced what we went through. The biggest part of being abandoned was you never knew what was going to happen to you from one day to the next. Today you might have something to eat the next day you might have to eat someone's food that was thrown away.

One day Ora (mother) told me that our biological mother had been walking up and down Crystal Street where we lived, looking for us. The neighbors had told, mother about our biological mother coming to their homes, asking if they knew where we were. This made me sad just to know she had been looking for us. I wish I could have just talked to her and let her know that I loved her. My heart was in turmoil between caring about Ora and our biological mother. It was hard to handle my feelings, so I just kept them inside me. Our biological father (Scott) had signed us over the State of Michigan, because they were not able to provide for us.

After the adoption we became officially (Murdock's). We never heard anything from the

King family or from our biological parents again. We had the choice of changing our first and middle names. My sister wanted her name changed to Laurel Jane Murdock and my brother wanted his name changed to Scott William Murdock. I left my name as Ruth Ann and added Murdock. I really thought that my name was all that I could keep that my biological parents had given me.

Somehow, life's journey can be much better and still have unexpected twists and turns. We started going to Hull Elementary school in Benton Township. I started the second grade. I learned to read with phonics, writing became easy, and I had no problem with math. I really loved school and looked forward to going and learning things I had struggled with before.

## *Chapter 4*

# So Many Lessons to Learn

Once again life had begun to change. We called Ora (mother) and William we called (daddy). Daddy worked for Auto Specialties in Benton Harbor, where he was a rank and file union member and a politician.

*Still Kicking*

*A very old picture*

It is my belief that William was a cousin to my biological mother. I have found that I have 14 cousins that are listed as Murdock's through my DNA with 23 and me. One of the Murdock's cousins is a second cousin through my DNA. I have checked with some the Kings to find out if there were any Murdock's in the King family and they said, no. This was very interesting information.

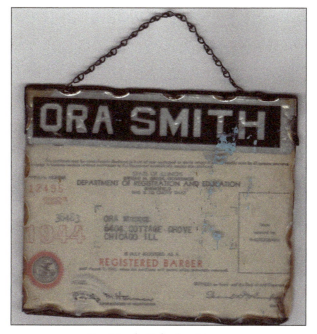

*Ora Murdock's barber License*

Ora was a very gifted barber, who had worked in Chicago with her sisters, Mary and Elizabeth. The barber shop was at 6404 and Cottage Grove.

She worked with Elizabeth and Mary, in the barber shop which was known as the "Three Sister's Barber Shop" in the late 1930's and 40's. They had sold the Barber shop and moved to the southwestern part of Michigan.

After we were adopted we found out that mother (Ora) drank. Her drinking became like putting gas on a fire in the forest. The alcohol totally changed mother's personality from loving and kind to being very angry. Nothing was out of the path of her anger mainly on the weekends was when she got alcohol. I loved her no matter what she said or did, she was my mother.

Mother (Ora) was an excellent homemaker. She taught us how to cook, keep house, and to work in the garden. The best foods we had were from the garden and there was nothing like the fresh vegetables especially tomatoes and green beans. Mother only gave us meat on the weekends for some unknown reason. The vegetables from the garden made for such goods meals.

During the summer, mother would get bushels of grapes, press them, let them ferment, and make her own wine. As the years passed, this became a major part of her life. Mother had no control of what did when she drank.

There were new challenges in the home, in the community, and at school that seemed almost too much. I used to just want to die because of all the problems at home and those from the past. The big problem was that we couldn't change anything in our life.

I remember when I was 10 years old our family became members of St Stephen's Episcopal Church in Benton Harbor. Daddy would take us to church, but mother would stay home. At home, things were tough, because more often than not, mother had been drinking. The challenge for us was to do everything right, so we wouldn't get in trouble. No matter how hard we tried it seemed we just could not please mother. When mother was really upset she would use her razor strap to make sure that you did not disobey her. Mother, could be a very kind person and caring person, when she was not drinking. She was very protective of us and very selective, when it came to those she would allow us to associate with as friends.

The best times were when grandmother (daddy's mother Lillie) would come from Mississippi and stay. She taught me to read my bible and to pray. When I was troubled about something I would tell her. In the fifth grade, I began learning to put my trust in God. God became the one source I could draw strength and courage from, to face unpleasant obstacles.

As time moved on, school became the most vital part of my existence. I stayed on the honor roll and learned how to lead. When I became captain of the Service Squad (safety patrol) this became a major accomplishment for me at that time.

*Chapter 5*

# A Loss

One morning as we were leaving for school there was an announcement on the radio. The newscaster said that Beatrice Jane King was found dead in a migrant farm shack in Sodus, Michigan of food poisoning. Knowing that she died hurt a lot (this was our biological mother) and knowing that she needed help and didn't have it. Our biological father had been the tuberculosis sanitarium for about four months at that point. We would not have been able to do anything for her that would have helped her. Daddy took us to her funeral that Saturday. There seemed to be an emptiness that we were unable to express. Her death really hurt. There was an attachment there. She was our biological mother and nothing changed that fact.

Janie and I shared a bedroom. Somehow at age 11, I found a bruise on the left side of my chest. One night I asked Janie did she think the bruise would go away? Janie didn't hear me, so I decided not to say anything else about the bruise.

One day I came home for lunch and Janie was home for lunch also. I always wore a sweater, because the bruise kept getting bigger. The bruise became a lump and I tried to cover it up. This particular day was different, I was 14 and my sister asked me about the lump under my sweater. I just simply said the lump was nothing. Janie told me to take off the sweater and let her see what that lump was. So I showed it to her. After looking at the lump, Janie said," either you are going to tell mother or I will". When mother got home my sister stood at the bedroom doorway of mother's room. I asked mother, do you think this lump will go away?

Mother was horrified and said I could have cancer. Mother immediately made an appointment with a surgeon. That night I prayed that, if was my time to die, I was okay with it. I was really tired of the struggles in my life. As I slept, I dreamed about a short curly headed boy. I wasn't clear about what that dream meant. The next day, they took me to the surgeon. The surgeon checked the lump and said it was not cancerous. When school was out in June for the summer, the surgery was done to remove the tumor. I was thankful that the tumor was benign.

I finished the 8th grade at the top of my class. Sometimes I wonder, what makes a person keep going, with all the failures, trials, and struggles. It seems like the kicks to the soccer ball (me) became more intense when I started high school in September of 1960 at Benton Harbor High I was 15. In high school, the requirements became more intense. I felt as though I didn't have the essentials mentally or the necessary things at home to compete with my classmates. With a deep determination, I kept going, because I wanted to graduate from high school. There continued to be obstacles at home that were affecting me and would make me want to say, "I have had enough, I'm tired". Through High School, I kept pushing myself.

There continued to be trouble at home. My sister moved to Detroit with a cousin and went to school there for a while. After a few months Janie decided, she wanted to graduate from Benton Harbor High School.

At that time, I had a part time job after school with Amvets, so I helped bring my sister back home. After Janie graduated in 1962, she moved out and married Robert Massengale. In July of 1963, they had a son Richard Massengale (Ricky died of heart decease in March of 2020).

I treated Ricky as though he were mine.

## A Loss

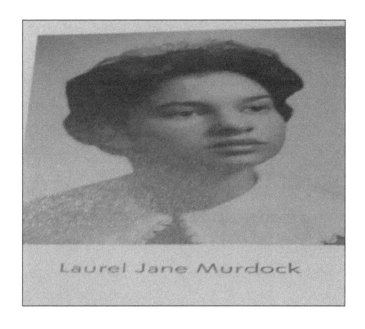

*My sister Janie*

One night my brother, Sonny, who was 16, tried to run away after he and mother got into an argument. I decided he wasn't going to run away by himself so I went with him. There was a couple that just kept picking us up. After they had picked us up several times, they notified the police and the police picked us up and took us to the police station. The police called daddy, who thought we were upstairs asleep. Sonny had to go to Juvenile court, because he was 16, and I was considered the adult who was responsible for him. This was not the only time Sonny got in trouble. When he was 17, he and some cousins tried to hot wire a car and wound up going to court. This time he had to face a judge. Our dad, the police officer was there who caught him, an uncle, who was a sheriff, and an Army recruiting officer was there. The Judge told Sonny, he had one of two options, he could either go to jail or you can join the Amy. After Sonny heard this he chose to go into the Army (January 21, 1964). Sonny was honorably discharged after having served two tours in Vietnam in June 1976 with two purple hearts. Sonny still has a bullet in his left leg and lead in his chest.

## A Loss

*Scott William Murdock (Sonny)*

In my senior year in high school (1963-64), I worked part time at Sears. In November 1963, Mother got drunk one Friday night and started fussing. Mother threw my clothes out of the house then she threw them back in the house. The next day, before I went to work I told my dad, I couldn't stay at home anymore. My dad was taking me to work, we stopped by Janie's and I asked Janie if I could stay with her and Robert until I finished high school. She said, I could, but all she had was a couch.

My Mother was upset and said, that I wouldn't finish high school, because I moved away from home. I had made up my mind that I would finish high school, and I would also go to the Junior college in Benton Harbor. I finished high school in June of 1964.

In September of that year I began to attend Lake Michigan Junior College, majoring in Liberal Arts. After I would get out of school, I would walk three miles in the rain, in the snow, and in the sunshine, to Mercy Hospital, where I worked as a nurse's aide. I had a hard time trying to earn enough money to stay in school so I went to work full time at a bindery that paid $.50 an hour. The unions were trying to get into companies so for some reason I was laid off. Mother became proud of me, and at one point she gave me the money I needed to pay my tuition.

In 1966, I went to work for Heath Company full time, in St. Joseph, Michigan in quality control. I was making $2.50 an hour which was much better. I still lived with Janie and Robert and gave them ($50) a week for rent and helped with Ricky. I bought my first car while I stayed with them (a 1963 Ford, Fairlane).

*Chapter 6*

# My Search

My church was a very big part of my life but I wanted to know more about the bible. I used to belong to a group called the Daughters of the King in the Episcopal Church. The ladies in this group were a lot older than me. I spent my 18th, 19th, and 20th birthdays with these ladies. The priest was always with us when we met. One evening before our group meeting I asked the priest if we could study the bible. He said, let me think about it and he would get back with me. Sad to say that never happened.

One weekend, in April of 1967, I went to a convent in Racine, Wisconsin with the Daughters of King. I wondered, what would it be like to be a nun? I was disappointed with my close friends and relationships. I felt like I was the soccer ball being kicked around and used. Things important to me were not important to those in my circle of friends. The convent was so dark and gloomy it did not seem to have the peace I was looking for. The priest was walking in the convent hallway. He greeted me and asked me how I was doing? I told the priest that I was trying to find meaning in my life and I wanted to find a purpose. He asked me if I had considered joining the convent? I told him, I would like to know more about the convent. He invited me to spend a week or two there. I told him, that I would have vacation time the middle of August and I scheduled myself to visit the convent for two weeks. We returned home after the retreat in Wisconsin.

I decided I needed to really find fulfillment in life but I just couldn't find it. One night I was driving home from my best friend Helen Mckenzie's house. I was so discouraged that I just wanted to drive into a farm's irrigation ditch on my way. In my mind I said, God wherever You are, help me. The thought of driving into the irrigation ditch immediately left me. I started, visiting different churches in Benton Harbor. It was a town with lots of churches of different denominations. Of all the churches that I visited not one had studies of the bible at least once or twice a week the Episcopal Church included.

One day while I was working on the assembly line at Heath Company, LaVerne Marsh and John Dillard were talking about bible studies at the Fairplaine, Seventh-day Adventist's Church. I asked how often would they have bible studies? They said, the bible studies were once a week. I then asked if anyone could attend the Bible class? They asked if I wanted to come to the bible studies? I said yes, I would like to come to the bible studies.

I started the studies the first week in August. After two weeks the studies in the book of Daniel answered many of the questions I had about the bible and history. I felt that I needed more bible studies to fully understand the way God worked in the beginning down to the end of time.

The lesson on Daniel, chapter 1 is about the choices Daniel and his friends made on their diet. They would not to eat the meat from the king's table. I had made a decision six months before I took bible studies to become a vegetarian. The vegetarian diet made a lot more sense to me.

Daniel chapter 2 is about Nebuchadnezzar's dream and the Image that represented the history of the world. The head of gold represented the Babylonian Empire; the breast of silver, represented Medio-Persian Empire; the thighs of brass, represented Grecian Empire, and the legs of iron, represented the Roman Empire. Finally the feet mixed with iron and clay represented the ten kingdoms that would not unite. The thing that caught my attention above everything was the hand that smote the image on the feet. The image showed how the end of this world's history would come. The hand was God's hand to let us know when time shall be no more. We don't know the day or the how, but we can recognize the signs of the time. As the stages of history have come and gone, even so shall this prophecy be fulfilled according to the Bible. After these lessons, I knew that I was going to join the Seventh-day Adventist Church. I accepted the Adventists message as truth from the bible, although there were areas that I needed to know more from the bible.

I had another friend, Lucy Mckinney who was a Seventh-day Adventist. One Sabbath, I called her to see where she was going to church. She said she would not be going to church in Benton Harbor, she said, but going to a tent meeting in Niles, Michigan. I asked Lucy if I could go with her, and she said yes. I had never been to a tent meeting before. This was really a very good experience for me to go to the meeting that Sabbath. There was one week left of the tent meetings so I decided to travel to Niles every evening after I got off work.

The last Friday, Pastor Aldwin Humphrey asked, who had intentions of joining the Seventh-day

Adventist the church I raised my hand. I had planned to join the Adventist Church but I wanted more studies. I was taken aside after the meeting and told what I needed for baptism the next day (September 9, 1967). Since I had planned on joining the Adventist Church, I committed to being baptized the next day. The service was wonderful and I felt that I had found the church I had been searching for. The speaker for that service was Dr. Mervyn Warren. I had heard Dr. Warren speak at the 2nd Baptist Church in Benton Harbor. After the worship service we traveled to Berrien Springs, Michigan. I was baptized at the Village Church. Dr. Warren's comment to me was that I needed to consider going to Oakwood College, in Huntsville, Alabama. Joining the Adventist Church was the best decisions I have ever made. This decision has helped me in every area of my life. The Lord has given me the purpose I was looking for.

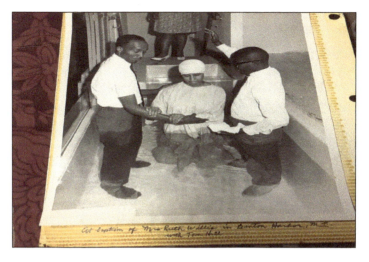

*Pastor Tom Hill, (Ruth Murdock Willis, baptized by Dr. Mervyn Warren) September 9, 1967*

At that point I wasn't ready to move and I didn't have the money to make a move to Huntsville.

In April 1968, I decided to visit Oakwood College. I wanted to see for myself what kind of school Oakwood College was. I went, not knowing much about getting a place to spend the weekend. I met some girls from Carter Hall, who invited me to stay in the dorm room with them for the weekend and that's what I did. I can't remember a lot, except that after worship service we had lunch with Doctor Mervyn Warren and his wife Barbara.

The fellowship with the Warrens was a wonderful blessing for me. The Warren's had three beautiful children (a boy Mervyn and two girls, Karis and Shawna).

The person we rode down to Alabama with had his car broke down on the way to Oakwood, in Nashville, Tennessee. That meant we had to find another way to return home. We took the Greyhound bus from Nashville to Indianapolis and then to Benton Harbor. I decided after that experience, if I were to travel anywhere, I would have my own car.

*Chapter 7*

# Time for a new Experience

After a while, I became interested in a new adventure. I decided to spend a week at the guest house at Oakwood University, and visit with the Warrens. I woke up to the smell of skunk and wondered what that strange odor was. They that was an odor I wasn't familiar with. I asked someone, they told me it was a skunk.

I went back to Michigan and decided I needed to put my finances in order to make a move to Huntsville, Alabama. I talked to a very close friend named Helen Carver, a member of the Berrien Springs Village Church and told her I wanted to spend some time in Huntsville, Alabama. Helen objected and she wanted me to consider Andrews University in Michigan. With reluctance Helen gave me a $100 for the trip. I resigned from my job at Heath Company in St. Joseph, Michigan and I proceeded to prepare for the move to Alabama. After making the decision to move to Huntsville and go to school at Oakwood College. I moved there to start a new life and advance my educational goals.

I found that there were finances I needed to get in school that I didn't have covered. I needed to find a job to earn money to pay my way. The only job at the time I could find was a job at Oakwood College cafeteria. This cafeteria gave me enough money to pay my car note and rent. I decided, I needed a position that would help me to be able to afford my living expenses.

Reflecting back, with a deep desire to go to Oakwood, I did manage to take two classes there. The first class was Introductory Psychology I can't remember who the teacher was. The second class I took was Life and Teaching of Jesus, the class was taught by Elder Johnathon Beal. One day Elder Beal was letting the students know how he thought they would progress in life. I sat quietly in my seat. Elder Beal looked at me and said I was going to marry a minister. At the time I pushed those words to the back of my mind. Sometimes life can have a lot of surprises without us knowing how God will work things out. Of all the things I expected to do with my life, marrying a minister was not one of my goals.

I love Oakwood University and I am so thankful that had the opportunity to take the classes I took there. Oakwood is a school of forever friends no matter where you go. The attitude of those who go to Oakwood is, everyone is that family, no matter how old or young you are. My suggestion to parents who have young children, is to plant the seed early in them to spend at least one or two years at Oakwood University. I wish I could have taken more classes there. I praise God for the classes I did take. I appreciate Dr. Warren for encouraging me to go to Oakwood.

## Chapter 8

# A New Experience

I applied for a position as a nurse's aide at Huntsville Hospital and was hired. I worked in Pediatrics and was given a two-year scholarship in nursing to Drake Junior College. The worst mistake I had made was moving in with a family that didn't understand my goals. They saw me as a way to increase their family finances, $55 every two weeks. I decided to apply for housing in the Nurses' Residence and was accepted. The rent was $25 a month. Huntsville was a place that seemed like a northern city in the south. It is a very progressive city that is constantly making improvements in education, science, and new construction.

One Sunday evening while I was working, someone brought me a post card. The post card was from my dad. The message on it said, your mother going to have X-rays Thursday. I called my Dad, and asked what is mother having X-rays for? My dad replied that she was having surgery Thursday. I told him, I would be there for the surgery. I requested immediate time off from work to go home. I purchased a bus ticket and went to be with my parents. I stayed home two weeks and almost lost my job. I went back to work at the hospital and was back in school. Everything seemed back to normal and I was finishing my second semester in Nursing.

One evening in December 1969, I called home my dad and answered the phone. I asked him how mother was. He said your mother is back in the hospital.

*A New Experience*

*William and Ora Murdock/ December 1970 at Mercy Hospital in Benton Harbor, Michigan*

I did not say anything else, or about anything I was thinking of doing at that point. I thought more of my mother struggling with cancer and Dad needing me than whatever my personal plans were.

Mother had given up alcohol in 1968, after I had joined the Seventh-day Adventist church. I had become very close to my mother she had objected to me joining the Adventist Church. But after I told her, how important bible studies were to me, she ceased to object anymore. My relationship with my mother had become very close, and she became my best friend. Mother and I could talk about everything and be comfortable. The Lord gives us time to make things right with those we have not always agreed with. I am so thankful that mother and I were at a different stage in relationship. We were able to express our love for each other before she died. We both found that we needed each other for reassurance and support in our trials, physically and mentally.

*Chapter 9*

# A LIFE CHANGING DECISION

Family was very important to me, but more than anything my parents meant a lot to me. My parents were the ones who taught me to make wise choices. I went to my room and packed my belongings and put them in my car. I moved back home to help my mother in her time crisis. During this time, I spent part of the week with my sister Janie (who died in 1985). Those days gave me the opportunity to help my nephew Richard, who was seven at the time (1970). The other times I stayed at home with my parents, assisting them. I took a position at Berrien General Hospital in Berrien

Springs, Michigan. I worked six months as a nurse's aide in 1970 at Berrien General and had to travel about 25 miles one way.

Considering the distance I was traveling to get to work. I decided to apply for a position as a teacher's aide with the Benton Harbor Public School System. I also decided that I wouldn't get involved with anyone who would distract me from church, my family, or my educational goals. This position was at the Martin Luther King School Building that January 1971. As a part of advancing my skills, I started taking classes in Elementary education. I was satisfied that I was in the process of reaching one of my goals and also being close to family.

On Mother's Day 1971 I went to see my mother, I was feeling lonely. Mother read my expression and asked, what's the matter? I said everybody has someone but I don't have anyone. My mother said she going to pray that God will send you someone to spend your life with. This was strange for her to say to me because I had never discussed with her wanting anyone in my life with her. I had thought the kind of person I wanted did not exist. The important thing for me was that the person would have to be a Christian, not only in general conversation, but in their beliefs.

*Chapter 10*

# NEVER SAY NEVER

Who, but God knows, the future plans He has for us. One Friday upon leaving the school, I walked to the parking lot with an associate teacher (Betty Washington). Betty asked me if I was seeing anyone (that was a strange question for her to ask me). I asked her why, was she was asking that question. I said no, and I wasn't interested in meeting anyone. This dear lady said, "I have a nephew, I want you to meet". I said I'm not interested in meeting anyone. Well, Betty was not giving up and we stood in the parking lot an hour and a half. Betty really was trying to convince me to meet her nephew. I kept telling her I was not interested in meeting anyone. She was very determined in her efforts and was not going to give up. I finally said," okay, I'll meet him". That was the second week of February 1972. The only kind of male friends I wanted were ones whom I considered like brothers.

I decided meeting him would not interfere with my family or with my plans for my future. This was my thought for any friendships I made. I had decided that no one was going to occupy my attention or distract me from putting up my borders. But I was also lonely. I went to Betty Washington's home to meet her nephew the last Sabbath in February. Betty lived in Berrien Springs, Michigan, the community located near Andrews University. As I walked to the door, Betty Washington opened the door and Betty invited me inside and introduced me to her nephew, Charles Willis. At first, I thought, he must be her husband I didn't say that I just thought it. As I began to talk to him, he started talking about the Bible and the

Sabbath School lesson. He seemed to know a lot about the bible. Charles was very polite and I was impressed with him.

*Me and Charles at his Aunt Betty's April 1972*

Charles was born at Hinsdale Hospital, in Hinsdale, Illinois, June 7, 1945. Charles was drafted into the Army November 15, 1965 as a Medic. His tour of Duty was at Fitzsimmons U. S. Army Hospital in Denver, Colorado until 1967. Charles had come from Chicago where he lived to meet me. We went to Pioneer Memorial Church for Sabbath School and church service. After the worship service, we had lunch at his aunt Betty's. Charles asked me about where I lived, so I took him to Benton Harbor, Michigan where I lived with my sister Janie. After touring the Benton Harbor area, I took him back to Berrien Springs, said my goodbyes and left.

The following Monday at school, Betty Washington came to see me. Betty said her nephew wanted to see me again. I had learned, from the parking lot experience, that she was persistent, I said, okay, but not the following week. There was something very special about her nephew. Charles let me know, he was a Christian and that his Christianity went with him, wherever he went. At this point I decided that I would treat him as a friend and that was all there would be to our friendship.

The second Sabbath in March of 1972, I saw Charles for church service. That afternoon Charles' mother (Ruth T. Willis) and his older sister (Sally Washington) had driven from Chicago to meet me.

*This is Charles sister (Sally), Joseph, Brandon, Amie, and Justin Washington*

Charles' mother and sister were very friendly they asked me a few questions. I started wondering about meeting a part of his family and why they had come to meet me. This seemed so unusual I felt special like I was in a dream that was not clear to me.

Charles sister Sally decided to call his dad and introduce me to him. Sally gave me the phone so I could talk to his dad (Lee Chester Willis). Charles's dad said, "I'm your Papa now you can call me papa". My conversation with his dad was not what I was expecting. After speaking with Charles dad, I told Charles's Aunt Betty, that I needed to go to Chicago to the Shiloh Church to meet the person, I'm calling Papa. The next Sabbath, I went with Charles' aunt to Chicago to the Shiloh Church. Charles met me and took me to meet his dad. Charles's dad was very gracious he acknowledged me as a part of the family (a daughter). I began to wonder what Charles had told his family about me. His dad had accepted me sight unseen and I accepted Charles family. I wondered where what is this friendship was leading to. I wanted to keep Charles as a good friend. I was apprehensive about our friendship becoming something more in the short amount of time I had known him. The relationship seemed to be going in a direction that I had no control over. I began to reflect on the dream I had when I was fourteen. The dream was about a boy who had curly hair. Dreams are usually very short and often not of any serious importance. Most of the time dreams are often forgotten once you wake up. I remembered this particular dream because it seemed very real. When I met Charles, it seemed like a reminder of the dream I had. I believe the Lord was allowing me the opportunity to fulfill a plan He had for my life. The Lord has taken me from where I was to where He wanted me to be at this particular time. So many times we try to plan the direction we want to go. We must allow God to have control of our future.

*Chapter 11*

# A FRIENDSHIP TO TREASURE

By March our friendship was starting to become very special for me. I began to appreciate more and more the time Charles and I would spend together. After I'd get home from prayer meeting Charles would call me. We'd talk about prayer meeting. He was such a blessing to me. April came and we kept seeing each other on Sabbath and talking about our values.

One Wednesday Charles called after prayer meeting he asked me to be his girlfriend. I said, yes I would. As our friendship grew, so did our love for each other. Charles became very important a very important part of my life. The months of spending time together was becoming our history. I believed Charles was very special and I really wanted to keep him and his family close as good friends. As the months passed, Charles let me know he loved me.

In July of 1972, he asked me to marry him. This question was not what I was really prepared to answer. As a result it took me four days to decide to say (yes). I still had to consider my mother's health and my dad had signs of a limited memory. My sister was struggling to raise my nephew (Ricky) as a divorced single mom. My family was very important to me and this wasn't an easy decision. Once I decided to accept Charles marriage proposal. I needed to make sure my family wouldn't be hurt by my decision. With lots of apprehension we started planning for our future together.

Charles wanted to talk to my dad to ask him for my hand. The last Sabbath in July we went to see my parents. At this point my mother was still alive. She really liked Charles because he was very respectful.

My dad cleaned off the lawn chairs. Daddy knew what Charles was coming to say to him. Therefore he wouldn't come and sit down. Daddy went in the house and came out and went back in. Finally, my mother came out of the house and sat down with us. My dad continued going in and out of the house and coming out. Daddy really didn't want to hear what Charles had to say. He wasn't ready for the question Charles had come to ask him. After 30 minutes, mother called him, and said, "Murdock come sit down". The conversation started with daddy talking about Gary, Indiana, then about places in Chicago. Charles looked at me and said your dad was making me nervous. I knew after an hour it was time for me to change the subject. I said, "daddy, Charles has come to ask you a question". Charles began stating how he was trained that it was proper when you want to marry someone to ask the father for her hand. Charles said he had come to ask your permission to marry Ruth. At this point, daddy once again started talking about Chicago. Mother listened to Charles' question, but daddy kept talking rather than answer Charles question. Mother waited quietly and said "you have our blessing". Daddy said hesitantly" okay just so you don't take her far".

I had been going to Chicago for church every Sabbath since May 1972. I spent lot of time with Charles and his family getting to know them. Sally became like a big sister to me and she did not want Charles to be hurt. I fell in love with Charles and his family.

One week in August, Charles decided he was going to go to church with me in Benton Harbor. The sermon was about mission and choosing to serve the Lord in His Vineyard. As I sat listening, a voice said," he's supposed to be a preacher", I looked around but there wasn't anyone sitting near us so I continued to listen to the sermon. As we continued to listen, the voice said it again marrying that was not what I wanted. I thought to myself "I'm not going to say anything about that to him. We were invited to brother and sister Beck's for lunch, but they had to take some members back home. While we were waiting, the voice said "why, don't you see what he will say"? I looked at Charles, he said, "what's the matter"? I asked," is the ministry your calling". He asked me how I knew and you know, I said, the Holy Spirit told me. He said," well, I guess we'll go to Oakwood". I couldn't say I don't want to marry a minister because I had already committed to marrying him.

*Chapter 12*

# Setting a Wedding Date

P lanning for our wedding date, we had considered getting married in June of 1973. We went to camp meeting for Lake Region Conference as an engaged couple. I felt like I was letting my family down because I had always been there for them. I told Charles that I was afraid of moving away from my family and, if my mother died before I got married, I wouldn't get married. I was so afraid that my dad wouldn't be able to survive without me. Charles asked if I you wanted to move the wedding date up. I said yes. He said, how about November?

We set our wedding date for November 26, 1972, Thanksgiving weekend.

Charles mother said she and Sally and Charles younger sister Sharone had always wanted to plan a wedding. I was thankful for them because I didn't know how to start. The wedding day was set to take place at Shiloh Seventh-day Adventist 7000 South Michigan, Chicago, Illinois. There were several bridal showers. My sister Janie, had a lingerie shower, Sister Beck and Sister Thomas had a bridal shower for the Benton Harbor Church, and there was a shower at Heath Company where I worked. I started looking for a wedding dress at Margie's bridal shop in St. Joseph, Michigan. Sister Beck paid for the Invitations and the Bible (for the Bible boy). I asked my dad if he would help with the wedding. He said, "he would buy my shoes, and get his tuxedo". He was having a real problem with me getting married although he wanted me to be happy. I started feeling like I was deserting my family.

But I loved Charles and I wanted a family of my own, a husband and children. I asked my sister Janie to be my matron of honor. I asked Sally Washington, Sharone Bond, Glenda Willis, and Edith Willis, to be my bride's maids. I chose Ladonna Willis and Carla Sebro as the flower girls and Joseph Washington and David Willis Jr. as Bible bearers.

Charles's dad said that if my dad wouldn't come to give me away, he would stand in his place. I moved to Chicago the second week in November and stayed with Charles' sister Sally. I was happy and sad at the same time, happy to be getting married to someone, who loved God and sad to be leaving my family.

*Chapter 13*

# BECOMING A WIFE

The wedding was scheduled for 3 pm at Shiloh Church, November 26, 1972. The Pastor who was performing the ceremony was Harold Lindsey, the pastor of Shiloh Church. My family and friends had come to attend the ceremony from Benton Harbor, Michigan (my mother wasn't there, because she was too ill). The wedding ceremony began, I was sitting waiting and thinking about the commitment I would be making in less than an hour. Chester Stewart, a deacon, happened to come by and said jokingly, if you want to run, you'd better do it now.

There have been two important decisions I have made and they are both until death.

The first decision I made was to follow Christ until death or the Second Coming.

The second decision was to marry Charles, and that was until death do us part.

The ceremony began and everyone was in their places and waiting for me. Pastor David Willis began to sing a song I had chosen, "The Song of Ruth". Upon his completing this song, it was my turn to enter the sanctuary to "Here Comes the

Bride". My dad was by my side escorted me. He was there to give me away. That was scary and I was afraid of sharing my life with someone who would become my husband. This was a major step but as I walked down the aisle. Charles met me and took my hand and we walked up the steps to the platform together. I think we were both afraid so we continued to hold hands throughout the ceremony.

The Pastor began by saying, "dearly beloved, we are gathered together to join Ruth Ann Murdock and Charles Milton Willis II together in Holy matrimony." Then he asked, "who gives this woman to this man?" My dad stood up and said, he did and he gave me away. I was happy to become Charles life partner and sad to be moving into a situation that I had never been in before. Charles had become my best friend but this was more serious than just taking a walk in the park together. It was committing to sharing a lifetime together. As we began taking our vows, there was no turning back to going home and being single. This was a life commitment. Finally the Pastor asked, Do you Ruth Ann Murdock take this man, Charles Milton Willis II, to be your lawfully wedded husband until death do you part? I said I do. Then the pastor asked, Do you Charles Milton Willis II take Ruth Ann Murdock to be your lawfully wedded wife until death do you part? He said I do. The pastor then pronounced that we were husband and wife. The pastor said, "what God has joined together, let no man pull asunder". The pastor then had us face the guests and said, "by the power vested in me by the state of Illinois and the Seventh-day Adventist Church, I now present to you Mr. and Mrs. Charles Milton Willis II". After the marriage ceremony

*Becoming a Wife*

*Ruth T. Willis (Charles mom)
and Ruth A. Willis Charles and Ruth Willis*

*Ruth T. Willis (CharlesMom) Ruth A. Willis, Charles M. Willis,
and Lee C. Willis (Charles Dad)*

We greeted the guests in the church parish hall and thanked them for coming. My dad, nephew, and sister and friends left right after the ceremony. The weather was beginning to get bad and the roads were getting slippery. We ate, cut the cake, and pictures were taken. Then we left to go to Springfield, Illinois for our week-long honeymoon.

*Chapter 14*

# STARTING LIFE AS MR. AND MRS. CHARLES WILLIS

After the honeymoon, we went back to Chicago to live and work for a year. Charles had been working at the Ford City post office in the Chicago area since 1968. I looked for a position and found one at the Federal Reserve Bank as a money sorter. We stayed with Charles' parents in order to save money in preparation to go to Oakwood College the following August of 1973. This was a wonderful experience because I had never truly lived in a Christian home. Charles' mother and Dad agreed had committed their home as a place where even the children that were babysat were taught about Jesus. Charles mother taught me a lot about what was expected of a Christian wife. The first month of marriage was a time for making physical, financial, and emotional adjustments for our lives together.

Charles and I had decided to wait before planning on having children. Charles brother-in-law, Pete worked for Or-thro, so he recommended a specific birth control contraceptive when we first got married. I used the birth control as the directions stated. We were preparing for Charles to go to Oakwood, and working to save every extra penny we could.

One morning we were preparing for church. The zipper was not working on dress I had planned to wear. I started to get upset. I tried on another dress the same thing happened. It appeared I had gained extra weight.

Charles went into his mother's room and told her that I was not happy with my clothes. Charles also told his mom he thought that I might be pregnant. I apologized to Charles then started to cry because my clothes weren't fitting me. I had not considered that I could be pregnant.

Sally made an appointment for me to see her doctor. Charles met me that Tuesday me when I got off work and took me to the appointment. The doctor gave me a pregnancy test which verified that I was pregnant and he told me when the baby was due. We wanted children once we accepted this new information we were very happy.

In April 1973 Alumni weekend we all went down to Oakwood College. Charles and I were walking across the campus after church service. Elder Beal came running to talk to Charles asking about when he was coming to Oakwood to prepare for the ministry? After our conversation with him, we said, "how did he know who Charles was?"

A sad day for me was May 9, 1973. My mother passed four days before her 72$^{nd}$ birthday. Her funeral was May 13$^{th}$ her birthday. My dad arranged for the funeral with Robbins Brothers Funeral

Home. Mother's funeral was held at St. Augustine's Episcopal Church.

Mothers are very special people and I would truly miss mine. My dad would now have to spend the remainder of his days without mother.

The months passed quickly as we were preparing to move to Huntsville, Alabama, in August of 1973. It appeared that everything was falling into place for our move. There was one thing that was a problem: there was no available housing on campus. Charles and I made an arrangement to move to the projects to a one bedroom apartment.

Charles put in for his retirement from the post office, to assist us in moving to Huntsville. We rented the largest U-haul trailer and packed our belonging in it.

We moved from Chicago to Huntsville so that Charles could prepare for the ministry. We were leaving everything that we were familiar with to answer the call God had given us. There is a song that, Eleanor Wright wrote, "Do You Love God, More than Anything"? The challenge was to follow

Jesus wherever He leads, no matter what challenges you face. (We were starting a journey that would change our lives forever in our desire to follow Jesus where ever He would lead us).

## Chapter 15

# Our Time at Oakwood

In order for Charles to register for school, he needed to be able to pay his tuition up front. The money wasn't there. He had applied for the GI Bill, but he had to be registered for school before that would kick in. This was a challenge we weren't prepared for.

We had been in Huntsville about two or three months, when I started asking Charles about the Second Coming of Christ. I had gotten baptized without fully understanding that part of the Seventh-day Adventist message.

When I questions I had, I would ask Charles' dad about things I didn't understand. Charles would pull out one of his books and say read this book, it will explain it to you. One night I asked him to explain something and I said you can tell me faster than I can read it. Charles got frustrated with me he went in the bedroom and came back into the living room. He said, "you really don't understand, do you?" I said I don't understand much about the Second Coming of Christ. Charles went to see the Pastor of the Oakwood University Church, (Pastor Eric Ward) to find out what he could to do to help me understand. Pastor Ward gave him a set of twenty four bible lessons for me to study. After I completed the 24 lessons, Charles gave me 36 bible study lessons by Mary Welch. After all these lessons, I had a better understanding of the Second Coming of Christ.

One day while I was visiting Barbara and Mervyn, and we started talking about Charles getting into school. Mervyn is like an older brother. He asked If Charles got registered for school. I said no and explained the situation. Mervyn told me to have Charles talk to me. Mervyn gave his assistance and Charles was able to register for the fall semester. Barbara and Mervyn have always been a blessing to me. They will always be family and their children are like my nieces and nephew.

*pictured are (Charles, Barbara, and Mervyn)*

There were many blessing we received at Oakwood. Charles younger brother Philip was at Oakwood before we got there. Philip had started working for the campus taskforce and he suggested that Charles to apply it. Charles applied and started working in the evenings after he would finish his classes. Charles worked with taskforce until he completed his studies at Oakwood College.

There were two other blessings we received during our stay at Oakwood. The first one was named Crystal Ann Willis born February 2, 1974 she wasn't breathing at birth but God in His Great Mercy sent an Angel to give her the breath of life. When I first saw her, she was on an oxygen table with an oxygen tube taped to her head. Crystal has always been strong-willed, as she was in her struggle to live. Crystal started walking at eleven months and talking around fifteen months. Crystal now, at the age 47, is still a person of personal in strength in all her endeavors to do.

*Crystal Ann Willis and Sharone Ellen Willis*

The other blessing was our youngest daughter Sharone Ellen Willis was born May 18, 1975. There were no complications when she was born so the doctor released me the day after she was born. She was quiet and calm then as she is to this day. She has always looked at life in the positive no matter, the struggles she has gone through. She was walking at eleven months and talking at fourteen months mainly because of Crystal. Charles' Dad loved Crystal and Sharone.

Our children became the highlight of our lives. The blessing of having children made our lives so much better. Crystal treated Sharone as if she were a doll. The girls have shared all of their life experiences together. They treat one another'schildren as belonging to them.

*Crystal, Sharone and their grandfather (Lee C. Willis).*

## Our Time at Oakwood

Charles and I both grew in our Christian journey at Oakwood. There was a blessing that we obtained from being at Oakwood, which was called, the Oakwood experience. Pastor Eric Ward dedicated Crystal and Sharone to Lord. We love Oakwood University and the friends we made while we were there.

Charles completed his studies at Oakwood in 1976. Charles still had two and a half years of GI Bill left.

Charles applied for Andrews University seminary and was accepted. The problem we faced before we moved to Andrews University was the fact that there was limited housing. We ask the Lord to allow us to have housing in the married student's apartments. There is nothing too hard for the Lord to do for His children. But the Lord worked things out so that there was available housing for us in the married student's apartments.

*Chapter 16*

# OUR TIME AT ANDREWS UNIVERSITY

~~~~~~~~~~~~~~~~

August of 1976 we moved into Beech Wood married students' apartments at Andrews University. The cost of living was more than at Oakwood. I had not worked during the three years at Oakwood, but rent there for a married student apartment was $50 a month. The cost for a married student apartment was $250 a month at Andrews. Charles was able to register for the Seminary, majoring in the master's degree program in Church Administration. After checking our finances, we decided I would need to work.

I went to work at Memorial Hospital, working in Pediatrics four days a week, working the 11 to 7 shift. I worked that shift in order to be home with Crystal and Sharone during the day. Charles worked several different positions while he attended Andrews. Working and keeping the family together was a challenge. When we look back at our experience, we say it was only God's grace that gave us the opportunities we had.

My dad and grandmother were still living in Benton Harbor at the family home. Grandmother was having some health issues with her heart and dad was having memory loss and arteriosclerosis. There was supposed to be someone to come to the house to cook and clean but that was not happening. On Sundays when I would visit and I would clean the house.

One Sunday I took the girls with me to visit with them. My dad took my car keys and put them up. When I got ready to leave, the car keys could not be found. I called Charles to tell him I couldn't find the car keys, Charles jokingly said I guess you are going to have to stay there. Charles brother Philip was at Andrews at the same time we were. Charles called Philip, to have him take him to Benton Harbor. I told Charles that I was going to call EMS to have them check on grandmother. The attendant checked her and said grandmother (she was 89) had been having mini strokes all day. Charles came and got the girls and took them back to Andrews. I went with dad to the hospital and they put grandmother in the ICU. After grandmother was admitted I took my dad back to his house.

Upon getting back to Andrews, Charles got news that his dads' brother had passed in Chicago. I then called Charles' mom to see what I could do to help her.

Charles' mom thought, the funeral would be that Thursday. I told her I would plan on coming to help her that Wednesday. The girls and I went that Wednesday to Chicago to help Charles mother. We got to the house and I was immediately told to call my sister, Janie. Janie told me that grandmother had passed while I was on my way to Chicago. This was difficult as my grandmother and I were close. My dad was having memory problems which did not help matters any.

The funeral for Charles' uncle was scheduled for that Thursday. As we were leaving for that funeral, my sister called and informed me that I would have to make the funeral arrangements for grandmother's funeral. We stayed overnight in Chicago. That Friday evening I dropped Charles and the girls off at Andrews. I then went to Benton Harbor to make the funeral arrangements with Janie for grandmother's funeral. The funeral was that following Monday.

My dad was having so much memory loss that it was difficult to keep track of him. We decided he would do better in an apartment but that did not work. Janie and Ricky wound up moving to Atlanta, Georgia. Then Janie wasn't working so I decided to take our dad to live with her. Janie took daddy to live with Sonny, which was not good for him. He died four months after being taken to live with Sonny in Augusta, Georgia.

Charles finished Andrews in May of 1979, without any distractions or stopping because of a lack of finances. After Charles finished Andrews, he was not hired by a conference. We put our things in storage and moved in with Charles parents until he got hired in the ministry.

*Chapter 17*

# Partnership with Jesus in Lake Region Conference

June 7, 1979, his birthday Charles was hired by the Lake Region Conference. Charles was so happy he forgot it was his birthday until around 4 pm. Charles was not officially hired until August of 1979. The President of Lake Region was Dr. Charles Joseph. Charles was assigned to be the assistant pastor of the City Temple Church in Detroit, Michigan and the pastor of the London Church in Maybe, Michigan. I was asked to teach kindergarten at the Warren Academy building In

Detroit. The class I taught had 23 kindergarteners, two of mine. This was the best experience of all the times I've had the privilege of teaching in Early Child Development. The opportunity to teach my own children was my greatest joy.

We were supposed to be in Detroit for two years but after a year, at the discretion of the conference, we were to the Evansville/Jefferson District. The district was 119 miles apart in two different time zones. Fulfilling the responsibility for this district was a real challenge with two young children. In Evansville, I worked two jobs the first job was 11 pm-7 am at a nursing home. I would get off work, get cleaned up, and go to work for the Evansville/Vandenburgh school system from 8 am to 3 pm. I loved working in Early Child Development as an assistant teacher in Evansville.

After two years and nine months, the conference committee decided we needed to be transferred to the Peoria/ Champagne, Illinois district. This district was 96 miles apart, another challenge to perform the necessary care for this district.

Peoria didn't have a lot of job opportunities, so I started my own child care business in our apartment. The girls were in Wilder Wait elementary school in Peoria in the 3$^{rd}$ and 4$^{th}$ grades.

After 18 months, in January, once again the conference committee decided, it was time for us to be transferred to the Lansing/Jackson district.

*Chapter 18*

# Charles Teaching at Peterson Warren

After we had been in the Lansing/Jackson district for eight months, the conference president persuaded Charles to accept a position as a Bible/History teacher at Shiloh Academy. We waited for the conference president to give the exact date for us to start looking for housing in Chicago. The president stated that he would get back with us, but months went by and all we were told was wait. I'll get back with you. We tried to be patient while we were waiting for a response, months and weeks went by.

This opportunity looked like something Charles really was excited about doing. He would be the Associate pastor at the Shiloh Church. Charles greatest desire was to be close to his family. The conference president said he would ordain him if he agreed to teach at the Academy. Charles accepted this request to teach in order to get ordained after he had been in the ministry seven years.

Charles started having a urinary tract problem in May of 1985. His urinary track tube had torn. The head urologist for the city of Lansing Dr. Johnson was his physician. He had been treating Charles for a kidney stone. The urologist put a tube in him to assist with passing the kidney stone. Three weeks later Charles went into out-patient surgery to have the tube removed. The doctor then told me he put another tube in him. I was not very happy about Charles having another tube put in to replace the one he had for three weeks. In the out-patient recovery area all the other patients had gone home after they were no longer under sedation. Charles stayed in a sedated state. I became very concerned after he had been out of surgery for more than four hours and was still under sedation at 5pm. At 7 pm I talked to the doctor and asked why he was not waking up so he could go home. The doctor said he was going to admit him overnight and I could pick him up the next day, Saturday. The hardest part was when I saw the doctor the next day and Charles was still in a sedated state. The doctor said he was admitting him and would write an order for x-rays. Everything did not appear to be fine. Charles was hospitalized and it appeared that he was going to die. I felt there was no the reason for him still being in a sedated state. As I was driving home crying asking God to not allow Charles to die from the hospital.

I went back home to meet with Charles' mom and his sister Sally along with Sally's children that had come from Chicago. They had come to go with me, Crystal, and Sharone to the hospital. We all went there to be with Charles. The staff at Sparrow Hospital had tried to contact the head urologist for the City of Lansing to no avail. I finally called the answering service and told them that if something was not done for my husband, I was going to be in trouble and so were they. The answering service got in touch with an associate urologist. The associate urologist responded to my call from answering service. One of the associates came and tried to catheterize Charles to get the fluid out of his body. The urologist talked to me and Charles' mother and said he would put the dye in him and do the x-rays on Charles himself. After the associate urologist did the x-rays, he stated that either Charles would have surgery that night or early the next morning. I said I was not comfortable with waiting and requested that they would do the surgery that night. At 12:00 that night they did the surgery, which only took 20 minutes to repair his urinary tract tube. The Lord is so good! Charles was put on medical leave to recover from the procedure.

While Charles was on leave, we went to the Shiloh Church. The conference president was the speaker for that particular Sabbath and he announced that he was going to ordain Charles.

The next week Charles' dad went to see the conference president to confirm what he had said at church. Charles' dad also wanted to get a true understanding of when Charles was going to be ordained.

*Charles was ordained (July 1986) At Shiloh Church, in Chicago*

We went back to Lansing to find out that he would not be moving to Chicago. Charles was assigned to Peterson/Warren Academy in Inkster, Michigan, teaching bible and history for grades

9-12. Charles never received a confirmation letter of the transfer. We didn't have time to look for housing as school had already started. We commuted from Lansing to Inkster for 4 months every day.

After we had finally moved to Ypsilanti, Michigan Charles began to have chest pains. At first he thought he had the flu but it was a major heart attack. Charles' chest pains continued so I took him to Katherine/McCauley Hospital. The x-rays showed, he had had a heart attack. Charles taught Academy Bible and History for five years and had the privilege of teaching both our daughters. Once again I taught in the Early Child Development program at Peterson Warren Academy.

*Chapter 19*

# A TIME FOR CHANGE

After two years of teaching pre-school, I decided it was time for me to do something different. I went to work for First Federal of Michigan, working in Mortgage Servicing for seven years. In March of 1996, First Federal of Michigan was bought out by Charter One Bank. Everyone who worked for First Federal lost his/her jobs.

A month went by and for the first time in my life, I drew unemployment. I liked working in banking, so I went to work for Flagstar Bank for five years in Mortgage servicing. In January of 2000 I ended my work with Flagstar Bank having worked in the mortgage auditing department. We would go to Chicago once a month to visit Charles family. His dad's health was failing. The weekend before Charles' dad died on May 13, 1997, we had gone to see him. This was a sad time for us he was always the backbone of the Willis family. On Sabbath mornings he would lead the family in worship.

During these years Crystal had graduated from Oak Park High School in June of 1992 and went to Andrews University, majoring in Public Relations. Crystal spent three years at Andrews. She was not happy at Andrews and decided to come home permanently. Crystal's deep desire was to go to Oakwood University. I wanted Crystal to stay close to home and that was my big mistake. We should have allowed her to go to Oakwood.

*A Time for Change*

*Crystal Ann Willis Jones and Charles Milton Willis Jones
(affectionately Known as Chip)*

Crystal, is presently living Carmel Indiana. She has one son (Charles Milton Willis III-Jones), we affectionately call him Chip. Chip was born August 8, 2003 in Southfield, Michigan. After Chip was born they moved to Grand Rapids, Michigan to be close to us. Crystal has been married for twelve to David Alden Jones from Detroit for twelve years.

At the June of 2008 camp meeting, Charles older sister Sally died. We knew Sally's health was failing and that she would not make it. Sally was always very hopeful and positive. She was the one who kept the family connected. Sally and I had a special bond. She had become my sister and now she was gone. That hurt. Charles mother was in the long term care facility, we couldn't tell her, that Sally had die. We believe that when Jesus Comes, she will awake from her sleep.

*Sharone Ellen Willis*

Sharone had graduated from Peterson/Warren Academy and went to Oakwood University, majoring in Accounting. I didn't want either of our girls too far from us. The second quarter at Oakwood, Sharone started dating her husband to-be over our objections, she was 18 years old and this was her first time away from home. She got married July 31, 1994, and we had our oldest grandson (Dennis LeRoy Wallace III) born November 15, 1994 in Huntsville, Alabama. Tre' graduated from Peterson/ Warren Academy in 2012. To this day (Tre') is a wonderful blessing to us. He attended Oakwood University from 2012 to the present and Tre' is still working on finishing his degree. He is a hard worker in whatever position acquires. We are impressed with his desire to face the challenges that have come his way.

*Tre and his mother Sharone Ellen Wallace*

Sharone decided to move back to Michigan in 1995 because of the need to be close to family. While living with us, she became pregnant with her second son Stephen Isaiah Wallace, born February 3, 1996. Stephen was diagnosed as a juvenile diabetic at age 2. Stephen has not allowed his health issues to hinder him from reaching goals that he has set for himself. Stephen went to University of Michigan, with a full four year scholarship. Stephen graduated in 2018, with a degree in Public Policy. He presently works for the state of Michigan as a children's Advocate.

*Stephen Isaiah Wallace graduated from University of Michigan 2018 and his mother Sharone E Wallace*

On December 28, 1996, our one and only granddaughter Nadia Renee' Wallace was born in Huntsville, Alabama. Nadia has a special attachment to her grandfather. Whenever Nadia faces a problem, she always wants her grandfather to help her resolve some of her issues. Nadia graduated from high school 2015 and was accepted at University of Michigan in the fall of 2015. Nadia is in the process of finishing her degree in Elementary Education, she loves teaching young children and observing their mental development.

I had started working for Indiana Junior Academy in October 2015 as the Pre-K/Kindergarten teacher for the fourth time. Charles mother was in a long term care facility. We would go and to visit her every other month. Charles mother was 92 years old when she died. His mother and I had been very close to each other for forty-three years, not as in- laws, but as mother and daughter.

After twenty two years of being in an uncertain marriage relationship. Sharone decided that it was time for her to find her own path. She divorced her husband in February 2017. The blessing out of her marriage was her three children. The kicks in life can be harsh, but they can be great learning tools that will benefit us in the future. God is always ready to help us.

*Nadia Renee Wallace and her mother Sharone Ellen Wallace*

Charles pastored the Maranatha Church, in Detroit, Michigan from 1991 to 2001. The Southside Church in Pontiac, Michigan was added to Charles district in 1996. In December of 2001, Charles was transferred to the Grand

Rapids, Michigan where we stayed from 2001 to August 2005. I worked for the Spectrum Hospital Child Development Center as an assistant teacher. While living in Grand Rapids, Michigan I attended Davenport University. For two years my major was Business Administration with emphasis on Human Resources. When moved, I had six courses I needed to finish my degree. Charles was transferred to the Indianapolis area in 2005. At this point, I have 62 credits from Lake Michigan Jr College in Benton Harbor, Michigan, and about 40 credits from Davenport University. I would have liked to have finished my degree in elementary education. At this point I am satisfied that I have knowledge in several areas. I feel so blessed to have been able to get the amount of education I have. God has been good to me in my journey.

Charles was transferred to the Eastside/Muncie, Indiana district in August of 2005. He pastored these two churches for seven years. One of the blessing we received from the Muncie Church is a close relationship with Kindra Henderson we call her our niece.

While we were in this district, I decided to volunteer at the Glendale Junior Academy and Capital City church school. A position became available at the pre-school/pre-K at Glendale church school, known as IJA where I taught for 5 years.

## Chapter 20

# After Retirement

Charles retired from the active ministry in Lake Region Conference on December 31, 2011. Our journey in the active ministry has had its blessings and many challenges. We would not change anything in our experience, even sometimes feeling kicks to the soccer ball. Charles had a burden for the Philadelphia Muncie Church. The church had a very small membership he wanted to help it grow. Sometimes situations happen beyond our control and this was one of those situations. Charles ministry was one of working to lead souls to Christ.

We had decided that when we retired, we would stay in the location where we were living at the time. We have made our residence in Carmel, Indiana, since August of 2005.

After Charles retired, he voluntarily pastored the Martinsville, Indiana Church for 3 years to help the Indiana Conference. This was a very interesting experience, working in a conference other than Lake Region Conference.

After battling cancer for 37 years, Charles younger brother Philip Chester Willis died in 2018. Charles had been helping him with his two church district (in Robbins, Ill. and Gary, In.). Charles and Philip always had a loving relationship. We raised our children together and they all went to Peterson Warren Academy. Life has a lot of twist and turns and sometimes it's hard to keep up with all the challenges, but somehow you manage to do it.

Raising children can take a lot of work. but it is worth all the effort that you put into it. My mother (Ora) once said that family is so important and I have found that to be so true. I am so thankful for my husband, my children, grandchildren and great grandchildren. Being able to take time not only to know our grandchildren individually we were also able to assist in raising them.

One of the best things in our journey was that on May 11, 2019, in Detroit, Michigan we had the great honor of becoming great grandparents. Our first great grandson is the son of Stephen Sr. and Rakala, (Stephen Isaiah Wallace the II).They live in Detroit, Michigan. Children are a blessing of the Lord. We were blessed to have Stephen II, in our home for two weeks while his parents went to Cancun Mexico for a vacation.

Moving forward we have a second great-grandson from Nadia and Maxon, (Maxon Ray Mathurin) born March 6, 2021.We are looking forward to meeting him on May 29th, in Florida.

Little Maxon "Children are an heritages from the Lord".

It is an awesome responsibility to raise children to be honest and respectful. "It truly takes a village to raise a child" Hillary Clinton. I have loved teaching young children and watching their mental development over the past fourteen years.

As I conclude my story, there has been one more addition to our family. Sharone married, Damon Ray Bennet, on May 30, 2021 in Winter Park, Florida. My prayers are that they will have a long and happy marriage.

It is my prayer that my story will help you to remain strong, when you feel like you have been kicked around like a soccer ball. In this life we all have things that will test us. But don't' give up put your trust in the God of the universe. There is one thing I want to also say Jesus is Coming. We do not know when, but be assured He is Coming. Study your bible and pray.